MEL BAY ... S
CHRISTMAS CAROLS ... O
MADE EASY
BY GAIL SMITH

1 2 3 4 5 6 7 8 9 0

Visit us on the Web at www.melbay.com — E-mail us at email@melbay.com

CHRISTMAS CAROLS FOR PIANO MADE EASY
arranged by Gail Smith

Table of Contents

Dedicated to Erika Hall

We Wish You a Merry Christmas

Traditional English Carol
arr. by Gail Smith

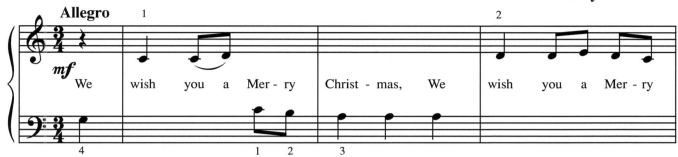

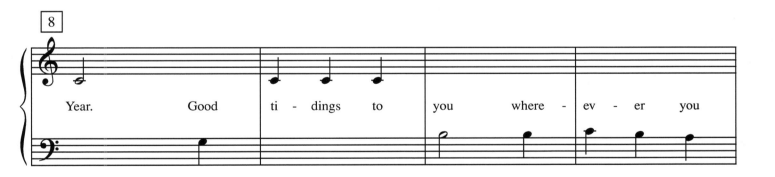

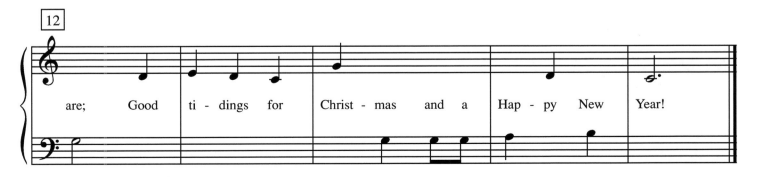

3

Dedicated to Ellie Kastelein

We Three Kings

arr. by Gail Smith

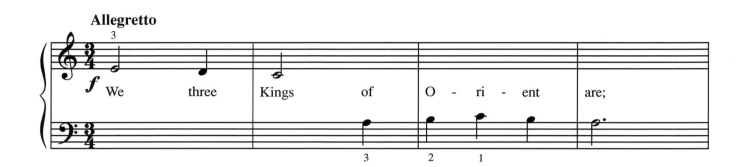

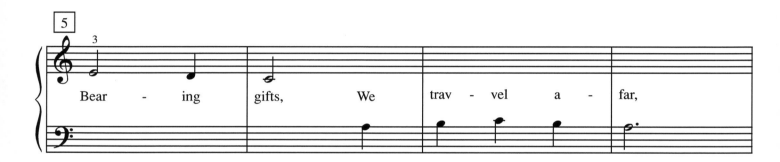

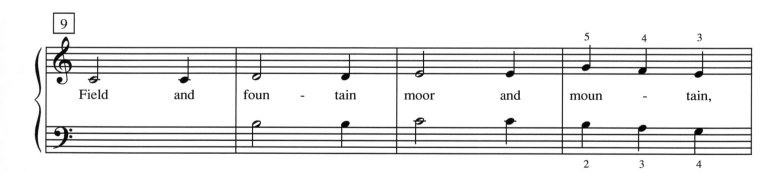

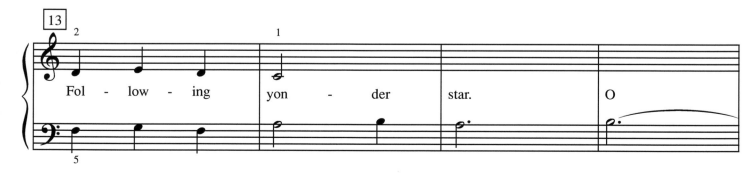

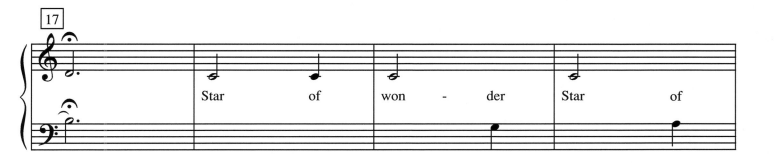

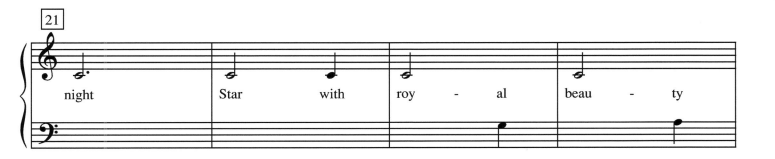

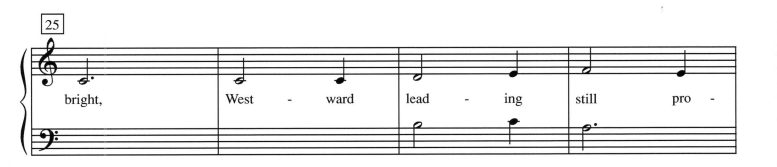

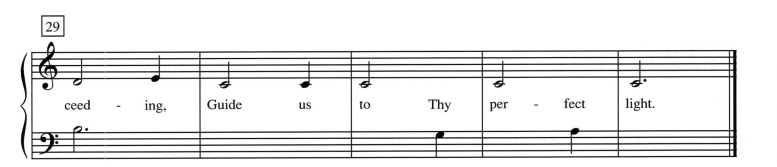

5

Dedicated to Emily Bishop

Away in a Manger

arr. by Gail Smith

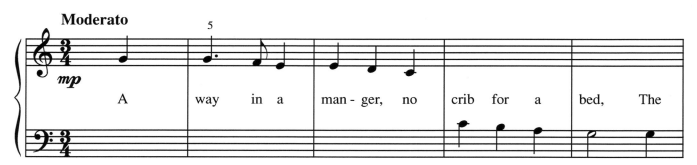

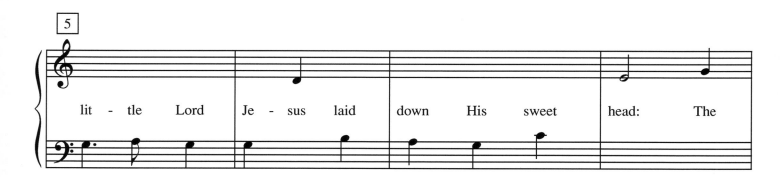

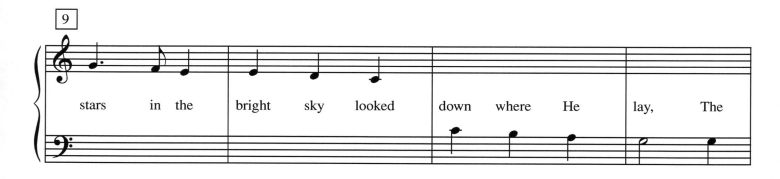

Dedicated to Anita Blackmon

O Come All Ye Faithful

Latin Hymn
arr. by Gail Smith

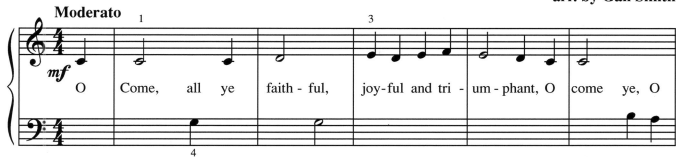

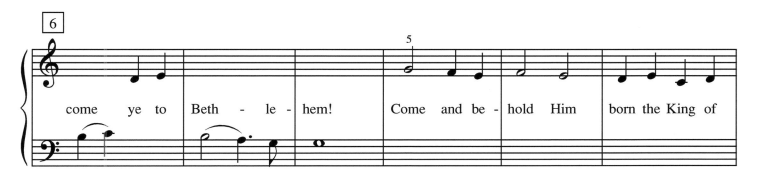

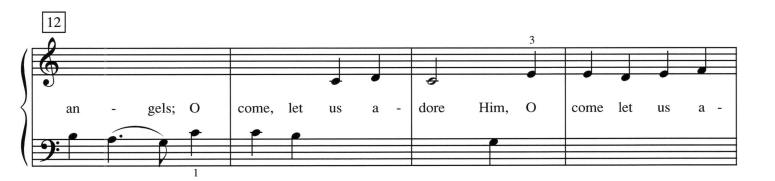

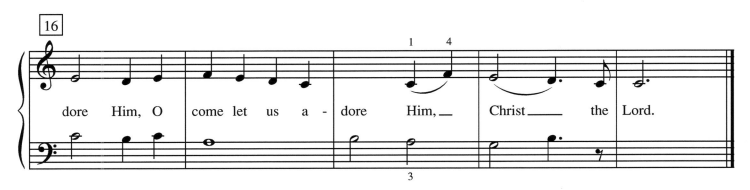

Jingle Bells

Traditional
arr. by Gail Smith

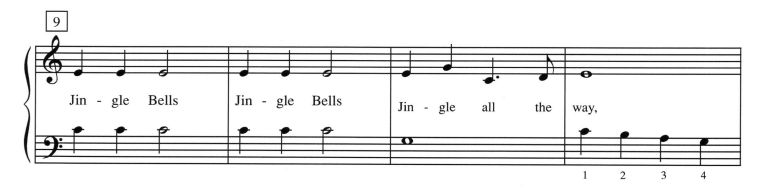

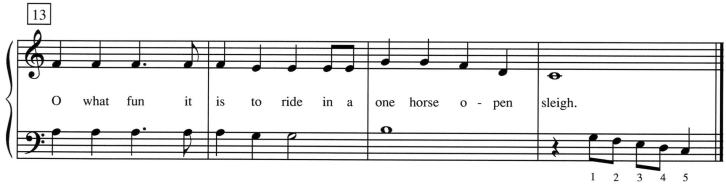

Dedicated to Lucas Smeets

The First Noel

Traditional English Carol
arr. by Gail Smith

Dedicated to Greta Worden

Silent Night

Franz Gruber
German Carol
arr. by Gail Smith

Dedicated to Alex Hall

Deck the Halls with Boughts of Holly

Traditional English Carol
arr. by Gail Smith

Moderato

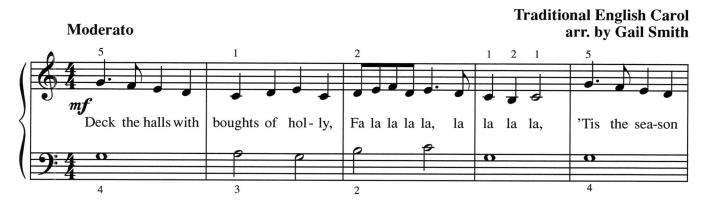

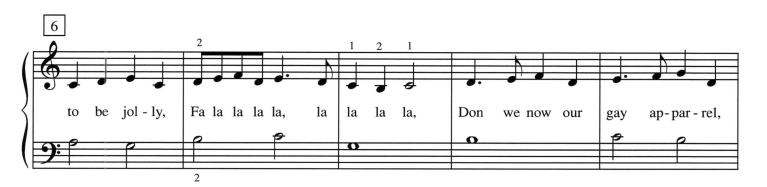

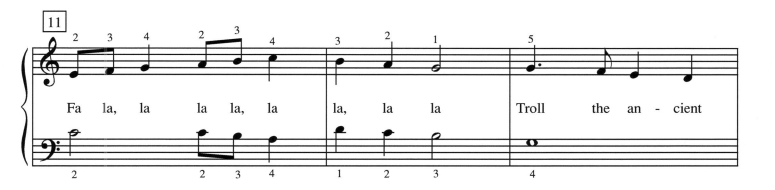

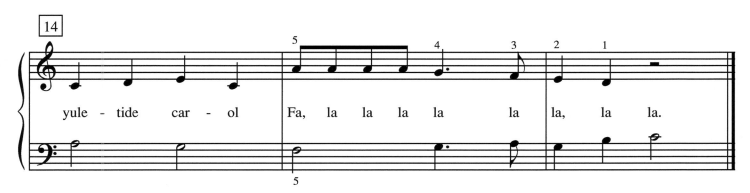

Dedicated to Greta Worden

Hark! The Herald Angels Sing

Felix Mendelssohn
arr. by Gail Smith

Dedicated to Donna Donato

Angels We Have Heard On High

French Carol
arr. by Gail Smith

Dedicated to Alex Hall

O Christmas Tree

Traditional German Carol
arr. by Gail Smith

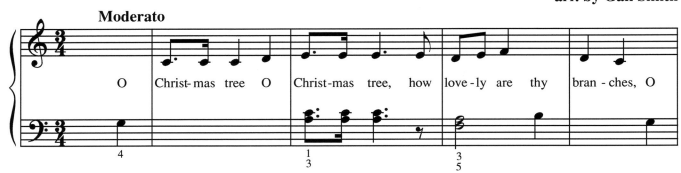

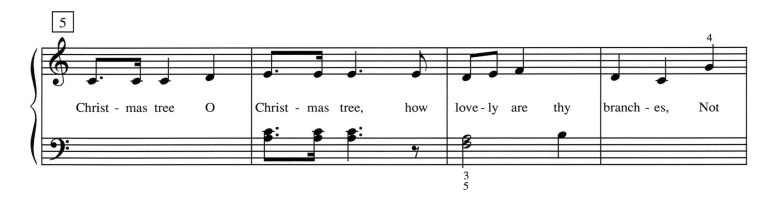

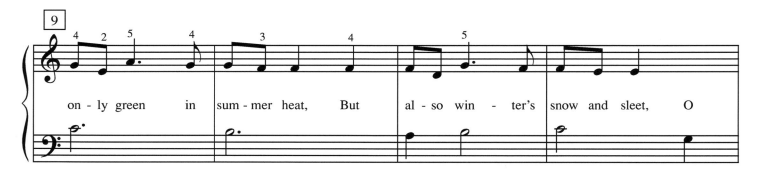

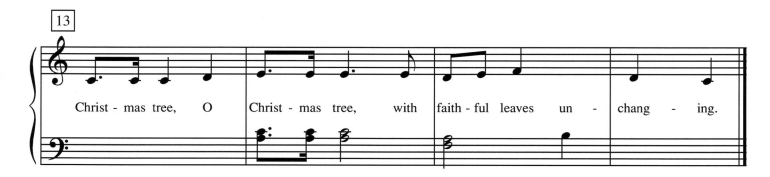

Dedicated to Kitt Curtis

It Came Upon a Midnight Clear

Richard Willis
arr. by Gail Smith

Dedicated to Elisabeth Crane

Joy To The World

G. F. Handel
arr. by Gail Smith

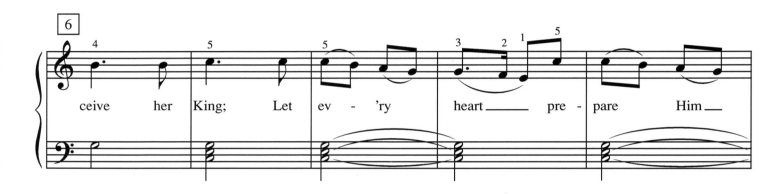

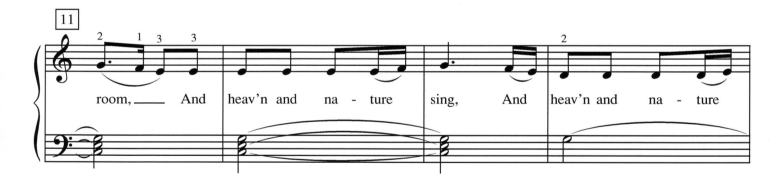

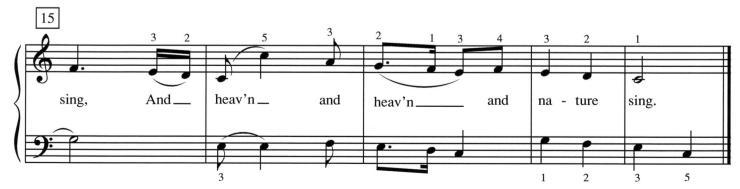